Kimberly
PRESTON

KIMBERLYPRESTON.COM

INTRODUCTION

How amazing is it that every time we read the Bible we see something different that we hadn't seen before.

If you've ever heard the Bible referred to as "The Living Word," this is why. It's what makes God's Word personal and applicable. It's not an ancient history book written by men who are now dead and gone. It's HIStory written by those who knew God and His Son intimately and allowed themselves to be inspired. The same Holy Spirit who guided the faithful writers of the Bible, guides each of us today as we hear from Him through His word and personalize these biblical principles to our lives.

I believe everyone has God orchestrated, inspirational stories within them. I've shared some of mine with you, and now it's your turn to share some of yours. You may think you don't have enough to write about to fill the pages of this journal, but trust me – you will. When you open yourself up to God's Word (for the first time or the millionth time), the Holy Spirit will awaken your heart to words and feelings you never knew you had. At least that's how it worked for this child of God, and as we are all equal in our Fathers eyes – I bet it works that way for you too.

So crack open your Bible and start with any book you want. God's Word is always reliable, so you can't go wrong. Read the whole book of Proverbs or a few chapters or just a small portion of a chapter. Read it until it's real to you. The goal is not to check reading the Bible off your to-do list, the goal is to hear from The Lord and let Him show you how close He truly is. He will speak to your heart as you read, and when He's given you something you want to hold on to – write it down.

The journal prompt questions may help, but if it's not what God has for you to write about – cross it out (or if you're like me, draw some ivy or flowers over the question to keep things looking pretty). Fill up the pages in one sitting, or leave room for more verses and stories for the next time you revisit that book of the Bible. If you run out of room, use the additional pages provided at the end of this book. This is your journey in your journal, so make it yours. I've left spaces for you to title and date your personal experiences as well as words that serve as themes to that particular Book of the Bible. Add more words as you grow in the knowledge you are given. And lastly, choose the verse or verses that feel like God is speaking directly to you - because He is. My prayer for you is that you enjoy this experience of letting God love you.

Ready-Set-Grow!

GENESIS

LIES

CONSEQUENCES

CREATION

SIN

TITLE

TRUST

Is there an event in your life that appeared harmful, but now you can see that God used it to accomplish something good?

SCRIPTURE VERSE

EXODUS

STUBBORNNESS
DISAPPOINTMENT
COMMUNITY
LEADERSHIP
FREEDOM

What plague in your life took (or will take) a miracle to overcome?

LEVITICUS

SACRIFICE HOLINESS SYMBOLISM PLEASING JUBILEE

Has God ever freed you from something in your life that was holding you back?

_____
_____
_____
_____
_____
_____
_____
_____
_____
_____
_____
_____
_____
_____
_____
_____
_____
_____
_____

NUMBERS

PERSEVERANCE *FOLLOWING* *FAITHFULNESS* *HARDSHIPS* *LEADING*

Have you ever experienced a time when you truly believed that God had something for you, but you couldn't see how it would be possible?

DEUTERONOMY

OBEDIENCE   HONORING   REVERENCE   RELATIONSHIP

GIVING

Using one of the Ten Commandments, describe an experience you had in regards to obedience.

_____
_____
_____
_____
_____
_____
_____
_____
_____
_____
_____
_____
_____
_____
_____
_____
_____
_____
_____
_____

JOSHUA

COURAGE DETERMINATION GUIDANCE DELIVERENCE PEACE

Share a time in your life when you had to be courageous as a parent, or as a child, or as a friend.

_____
_____
_____
_____
_____
_____
_____
_____
_____
_____
_____
_____
_____
_____
_____
_____
_____
_____
_____
_____
_____
_____
_____

JUDGES

SEEKING · EMPOWERMENT · LOYALTY · TESTING · CLARITY

Have you ever asked God to send you a sign while making an important decision? Did He?

RUTH

DEDICATION PROVIDENCE KINDNESS PROVISION REDEMPTION

Has God ever provided for you in an unexpected way?

___
___
___
___
___
___
___
___
___
___
___
___
___
___
___
___
___
___
___
___
___
___
___
___

1 & 2 SAMUEL

DESPERATION

DISAPPOINTMENT

SURRENDERING

TRUST

HUMILITY

Share a time of when you let go of something of value to you.

1 & 2 KINGS

SOVEREIGNTY

CONFLICT

DISRUPTION

HOPELESS

GROWTH

Can you think of a time in your life when God took something very small and used it to accomplish something very big?

1 & 2 CHRONICLES

LISTENING · INTENTIONAL · TESTIFYING · ACCEPTING · SEEKING

What are your thoughts and feelings on the idea of God speaking to you or through you?

EZRA

RESTORATION · OPEN-MINDED · PERSPECTIVE · REBUILDING · FAITHFUL

Tell of a time God used your disappointment to become your joy.

NEHEMIAH

OBSTACLES

OVERCOMING

PRUDENT

GRACIOUS

LISTENING

Is there a new perspective on a grim situation that you need to ask God for?

ESTHER

PATIENCE DELIVERANCE INFLUENCE WISDOM

TIMING

Is there someone in your life who you wish would know the love of Jesus? What are some ways you could show this love with a subtle glow?

_____
_____
_____
_____
_____
_____
_____
_____
_____
_____
_____
_____
_____
_____
_____
_____
_____
_____
_____

JOB

PERSEVERANCE

SUFFERING

SADNESS

CHANGE

BLESSING

What has been the hardest trial of your life thus far? Can you see where God was in it?

PSALMS

HEARTFELT **EXPRESSION** **PRAISE** **LAMENT** **WORSHIP**

Choose a psalm that speaks to you, then write a personal poem, prayer, or letter to the Lord expressing your pain, your praise, or perhaps both.

PROVERBS

INSTRUCTIONAL

PROBABLE

WISE

PRACTICAL

PRUDENT

Find a proverb that inspires you and tell why.

_____
_____
_____
_____
_____
_____
_____
_____
_____
_____
_____
_____
_____
_____
_____
_____
_____
_____
_____
_____
_____
_____

ECCLESIASTES

PERSPECTIVE

MEANINGFUL

UNCONTROLLABLE

IMMORTALITY

FREEDOM

How does God give meaning to the life you were given?

___
___
___
___
___
___
___
___
___
___
___
___
___
___
___
___
___
___
___
___
___
___
___

SONG OF SONGS

LOVING
REFLECTIVE
EXPRESSIVE
PASSIONATE
VISUAL

What is the song that sings to your heart
and brings you peace and joy?

ISAIAH

PROPHETIC FULFILLMENT GLORIFYING HOPE RESCUING

Have you ever prayed a prayer or encouraged another with words that did not feel like your own?

JEREMIAH

CALLED
GRACE
ALL-KNOWING
JUDGMENT
EQUIP

What do you think God has created and *set you apart* for?

LAMENTATION

INEXPRESSIBLE · *INQUIRING* · *SHAME* · *RECOLLECTING* · *SORROW*

Write God an honest letter. It's okay to lament and be real with Him about your pain or frustration. Let it out and then sit quietly, allowing Him to fill you with compassion and peace. He will not fail you.

_____
_____
_____
_____
_____
_____
_____
_____
_____
_____
_____
_____
_____
_____
_____
_____
_____
_____
_____

EZEKIEL

WATCHFUL
REMOVAL
VISION
WARNING
CARING

Are there any people in your life who you serve as a shepherd to? Are you caring well for your flock?

DANIEL

BOLDNESS

MIRACULOUS

OPPOSITION

UNWAVERING

TESTING

Is the Lord's presence known in your home? How do you proclaim Him? Or how could you start?

_____
_____
_____
_____
_____
_____
_____
_____
_____
_____
_____
_____
_____
_____
_____
_____
_____
_____
_____
_____

HOSEA

REBELLION · **UNCONDITIONAL LOVE** · **SYMBOLIC** · **UNFAITHFUL** · **HEARTACHE**

Is there anyone in your life who is hard to love? Could you possibly love them through the eyes of the Lord?

JOEL

FORGIVENESS

DELIVERANCE

CONFESSION

MERCY

CRISIS

Have you ever experienced a time where God mercifully spared your life, or the life of someone you love?

AMOS

IGNORANCE · SELF-RIGHTEOUSNESS · JUST · ACCEPTING · LOVE

Whom do you love that is most different from you?

_____
_____
_____
_____
_____
_____
_____
_____
_____
_____
_____
_____
_____
_____
_____
_____
_____
_____
_____

OBADIAH

BETRAYAL DISASTROUS HEALING HOPE PRIDEFUL

Has your own family ever had to rise above difficult circumstances? How was this accomplished?

JONAH

GRACE
FLEEING
CONSEQUENCES
OBEDIENCE
DISREGARD

Is there a tug on your heart regarding something you have often felt you were called to do, but have never done it? What would it take to make that happen?

MICAH

DESTRUCTION · REDEMPTION · VIGILANT · FUTURISTIC · ANTICIPATE

Write a personal letter to the hope that lies within you.

NAHUM

GRIEVED
ENDURE
STRONGHOLD
WRATH
BELIEVE

How has God been your refuge in times of trouble?

HABAKKUK

CONFUSION · UNFATHOMABLE · VULNERABLE · TRUST · HONESTY

What are your thoughts on being angry with the Lord? Are there forms of appropriate and inappropriate anger toward Him?

ZEPHANIAH

WICKEDNESS

TRANSFORMATION

DISASTER

PURIFY

WORSHIP

Can you imagine what it must feel like to sing alongside the Lord? What do you think His voice might sound like?

HAGGAI

RENEWAL

COVENANT

SUCCESS

BLESSING

PRIORITY

In what way do you or could you use your personal space to bring God glory?

ZECHARIAH

DISCOMFORT REJECTION DELIVERANCE GROW LEARN

Is there an old notion from the past that you were able to overcome? Or perhaps one that you'd like to?

MALACHI

DISPUTES • SELFISHNESS • OFFERING • ABUNDANCE • INSPIRING

Has God ever thrown open the floodgates and blessed you more than you could have imagined?

_____
_____
_____
_____
_____
_____
_____
_____
_____
_____
_____
_____
_____
_____
_____
_____
_____
_____
_____
_____
_____
_____

MATTHEW

PRAISE · RELATIONAL · YIELD · ASK · REPENT

Write a personal prayer to God using the Praise, Repent, Ask, Yield template.

MARK

INTERCEDING · *WILLINGNESS* · *CHRISTLIKE* · *COMMUNITY* · *SERVANT*

Make a list of people you could be in prayer for as well as a specific concern about each one that you would like to bring to the Lord. Visit this list often, and add the date and how God answered that prayer over time. Remember: even a "no" or a "not yet" is still an answer to prayer.

_____
_____
_____
_____
_____
_____
_____
_____
_____
_____
_____
_____
_____
_____
_____
_____
_____
_____

LUKE

BELIEF

WATCHFUL

COMPASSION

FULFILLMENT

SAVIOR

What has God done in your life lately that you have forgotten to thank Him for?

JOHN

GOOD NEWS · *REMEMBRANCE* · *DISCIPLE* · *FORETOLD* · *WORKS*

Who in your life has impacted you in such a way that you can't help but want to make them known to others? Afterwards, reflect on the impact of Jesus' sacrifice for you.

_____
_____
_____
_____
_____
_____
_____
_____
_____
_____
_____
_____
_____
_____
_____
_____
_____
_____
_____
_____

ACTS

WITNESS

INVITING

EVANGELIZE

HELPER

GO

What unlikely place could you bear witness to your faith in Jesus? Or have you already?

ROMANS

DIVISION RIGHTEOUSNESS HUMILITY GLORIFY

UNITY

As a church, God desires us to come together, each exercising the gifts that have been given to us. What unique gift has God given you the ability to do? How can you use this gift to glorify Him?

1 & 2 CORINTHIANS

RECONCILIATION

REALIZATION

COMMITMENT

CORRECTION

GENEROSITY

Look inside your clay jar and ask the Lord to show you the treasures He's hidden within you.

GALATIANS

LOVE
FAMILY
JUSTIFIED
FREEDOM
CARE

Tell of a time that someone helped you carry a burden or perhaps a burden of someone else's that you helped them carry.

EPHESIANS

DISCOVERY · UNIFICATION · ABUNDANCE · JOY · FAITHFUL

Can you think of a time in your own life when the Lord gave you *immeasurably more than you asked or imagined?*

PHILIPPIANS

UNDERSTANDING

PERSPECTIVE

LIFE

POSITIVITY

CONNECTION

Write out your thoughts and possibly an experience that you have had in regards to Paul's statement in Philippians 1:21 *To live is Christ, but to die is gain.*

COLOSSIANS

KNOWLEDGE

FALSE TEACHERS

DEVOTION

PROCLAIM

PRAYER

Reflect upon your own household. Do you or your family members struggle with submitting, loving, or obeying? Seek God's peace in surrendering the struggle to Him.

1&2 THESSALONIANS

ENCOURAGEMENT

COUNTER-CULTURAL

MOTIVATION

DETERMINATION

POSITIVITY

Think of something you dread doing and play the Gratitude Game the next time you have to endure it. How did that turn out for you?

1&2 TIMOTHY

ENDURANCE · **SELF DISCIPLINE** · **TEACHABLE** · **BOLDNESS** · **WISDOM**

What gift has God given you that you feel called to fan into flame? What ways could you do that?

TITUS

EXEMPLARY
EMPOWERMENT
AUTHENTICITY
SELF-CONTROL
GOODNESS

Is there an important life skill or concept that did not come easy to you? Is there someone who shepherded you into developing it?

PHILEMON

REFLECTIVE
RECONCILIATION
KINDNESS
PEACE
PRUDENT

Can you think of a situation in your life that you've had to make peace with? How did you do this?

HEBREWS

PERSECUTION · STEADFAST · TRUSTING · EVER-PRESENT · HARDSHIP

What is an area in your life where God has clearly been faithful? Are you going through a hardship now that is requiring you to trust that God will be faithful yet again?

JAMES

STRENGTH
INTEGRITY
PERSEVERANCE
OBEDIENCE
PATIENCE

Have you ever faced a trial that tested your faith? Looking back would you say this experience deepened or weakened your walk with the Lord?

1 & 2 PETER

IDENTITY
RESPONSIVE
HOPEFUL
GENTLE
HOSTILITY

What new hope or new identity do you cling to despite any opposition this world brings?

1,2,3 JOHN

FELLOWSHIP

SELF-SACRIFICING

HOSPITABLE

LOVE

DEEDS

Who is the best example in your life of *Love-in-action*? Why do you feel that way?

JUDE

DECEIVING

PROTECTION

IDENTITY

JUDGMENT

CONDUCT

Have you ever said or done something out of your comfort zone and found that it brought God glory?

REVELATION

PROPHETIC · **UNVEILING** · **SEALED** · **SYMBOLIC** · **WARNING**

Is your name written in the Lamb's Book of Life? Write the names of those you hope to share eternity with. Ask the Lord to work through you in witnessing to others through prayer, your words, and your example.

www.ingramcontent.com/pod-product-compliance
Lightning Source LLC
Chambersburg PA
CBHW072157200426
43209CB00052B/1334